Recharge Your Business in 120 Days
By Laura Gallagher

THE CREATIVE COMPANY • MADISON

#180 (in) 120

Copyright © 2016 by Laura Gallagher

Cover photo by Bob Wydra
Book design by Jessica Nordskog

Printed in the United States of America

Third Printing, 2017

ISBN 1533218277

The Creative Company, Inc.
636 W. Washington Ave.
Madison, WI 53703

thecreativecompany.com
180in120.com

#180in120 is a registered trademark of The Creative Company, Inc.

Acknowledgements

In addition to the team that brought this book to life in a physical form and on the web, I'd also like to thank every client and every employee I've ever had the privilege to serve. I'm grateful for your investment in me and the opportunity to invest in you. Thank you for your ideas, inspiration, art and words.

About the Author

Laura Gallagher is the President and founder of The Creative Company, where she serves successful entrepreneurial companies and nonprofit organizations. In June of 2016, she was recognized by the Governor as a Trailblazer in Wisconsin. She founded the company in 1989 when she was a senior in college. Her firm, located in downtown Madison, Wisconsin, is in the top 4% of women owned firms in the United States in terms of number of employees and gross sales. She is also the founder of the start-up, Mathetria Press, a publishing company and a Regional Ambassador in North America for Women's Entrepreneurship Day.

In 2017, she continued her passion for learning and growing by applying for and graduating from Goldman Sachs' 10,000 Small Businesses Program at Babson College with a Certificate in Entrepreneurship. She is also a 2016 graduate of Harvard Professor Michael Porter's Initiative for a Competitive Inner City.

Laura's passion is people, music, art and words. She believes that one person can change the world or at least their corner of it.

TABLE OF CONTENTS

Preface

Introduction

I'm guessing you picked up this book because you're in a bit of a slump – maybe even a serious one. Or maybe you just want things to be different … the way you always knew they could be.

My hope for you is that you come alive again. Your organization, family and friendships will be better for it, too.

In sharing these stories, which include some pretty humbling moments, I hope you'll be invigorated. I really believed my sacrificial love for my brand and my employees was good for them, but it wasn't. I first had to love myself, my failures and triumphs and own it—all of it—before I could move forward again, before I could be really free to create at The Creative Company.

On that same note, I recently started studying piano with a fabulous teacher. I played well enough to perform, but there were some key elements I was missing. Because I hadn't studied music theory well enough to really know the language, I had to focus very hard on the notes to play them perfectly. There was no freedom in the music unless I had rehearsed it a hundred times and even then, when you play with others, many things can go wrong, and sometimes they do. Safety was missing because I didn't understand the language at a root level. For me to be able to play freely, I had to return to the fundamentals, to scales and chords, and become a child again.

In some ways, this is exactly what I did with my company. I stripped away the facade and got real with myself and everyone around me. I added in 100 percent accountability from every angle. I kept the truth-tellers close and I became one of them, as well. Instead of minimizing the challenges related to some of our systems and processes, I acknowledged them and asked questions such as, "What is essential for you to be ridiculously successful for our clients?" and they told me.

When you're in a position of power and authority, respect is a natural byproduct, but with that can come a false sense of self at times. To get anywhere, we have to get over ourselves and become learners again. That's where the real joy is anyway.

#180in120 isn't just the name of this book; it's a way of turning things around—a mantra of sorts that says to everyone around you and to yourself, "You've got this thing." There's something about a short-term goal achieved that motivates you to set another and another. Whether it's for business or your personal life or some sort of altruistic endeavor, if you're not satisfied with the way things are, you have the ability to change them to the way you always knew they could be.

I wish you well as you take this on and hope you'll write me about your success. The stories we read have the power to change us. I trust mine will impact yours in ways that will enrich you, your business and your life.

#180in120—The Choice is Yours.
What Will You Do with the Next 120 Days?

Share your stories by emailing me at
laura@thecreativecompany.com
or by messaging me on LinkedIn.
You can also follow me on Twitter
@creativecompany

Because the Best Brands are Built from the Inside Out

Over the next four months, I'll be writing about organizational change. Through a series of events, I feel as though the company I founded in 1989 has become less than it is capable of. Innovation has been slower than normal and we've lost our focus. We need to get back to "why"—"Why we are here?"

On May 1, 2015, I decided to give myself 120 days—until August 31—to see dramatic results with my company, a PR and digital agency called The Creative Company, based in Madison, Wisconsin.

We're negotiating on a new lease now and I have high hopes

for The Creative Company in 2015 and beyond. I want to make sure we're on track to hit our goals and help our clients achieve more than they ever thought possible, not just by being good or even great, but by doing good, too.

Last Monday, our exec team met for two hours in a conference room and had one of the best brainstorming sessions we've ever had. We talked about what we believe, who we are and what's holding us back. We talked about changing.

We haven't exactly been slacking off over the last five years. We've been recognized as one of the Best Places to Work in Dane County and honored with the Gold Award for Best Ad Agency in Wisconsin. We've won plenty of awards, in fact, and sales were up year over year and are up for first quarter of fiscal 2015. But it's a feeling in the air that needs to change. It's time to reboot.

One of the services we offer is a management consulting tool I created called "The Imagine Plan." It starts with a written plan that incorporates the company's vision and purpose into a manifesto and ends with action. The Imagine Plan is not something that sits on the shelf, but rather lives in the hearts and minds of the people who live it every day—your employees, customers and the community you live and work in. We've seen clients create healthier cultures and more focused organizations with better results, which netted them higher profits and increased sales.

It is our turn.

I'm never one to go alone for the ride if I can bring a small posse of extraordinary people along with me. I'm inviting you to join us on this journey.

For the next four months, I'll be blogging about the work we're doing to reshape this organization. I'll share it all—even the work that hurts. I was on a panel a few weeks ago and was asked, "What's your biggest barrier to success?" And I answered honestly, "I am." And I am. But I care more deeply about what we're trying to accomplish than the preservation of my ego so I'm asking for help. If you have gone through this process and have insights to share, I want to hear from you.

For clients, we follow Harvard business professor and best-selling author John P. Kotter's process for creating major change. Here are his first four steps.

STEPS FOR CREATING CHANGE

Step 1: Create a sense of urgency.

Step 2: Build a guiding coalition.

Step 3: Form a strategic vision and initiatives.

Step 4: Enlist a volunteer army.

Step 1 is establishing a sense of urgency, which we did at last week's meeting.

Step 2 is creating the guiding coalition to lead the change and getting that group to work together as a team. Well, they've been chosen and I'll let you know how well it goes.

Step 3 is developing a vision and a strategy, which we're going off site for. We'll be at the Madison Club, in downtown Madison, for a few hours tomorrow where we'll work on the "Why." We already know "What" and "Who," but as Simon Sinek says, "great leaders ask why," and it's our mission to discover and know it.

Step 4 will be getting a "volunteer army" on board— people who believe in the change.

My mission is to create, with the help of my incredible team, a company that is worthy of your attention. My goal is to create something worth talking about because it stands apart in the marketplace. My desire is to connect our values with our work. My hope is that those who have the same values will retain us to help them achieve their goals in the marketplace. I've always said the best brands are built from the inside out. This time, I thought I'd start with my own.

Thanks for coming along on this journey and for being part of my peer network that has helped The Creative Company become what we are. The best, however, is yet to come.

#180in120—The Choice is Yours.
What Will You Do with the Next 120 Days?

Why the Elephant in the Room
Needs to Be Set Free

On Tuesday, May 5, 2015, we held our first off-site retreat since 2012. I was really looking forward to it. I wanted to show my team that it was a new day—not just with our words but also with our location. I also wanted them to know how valued they are, so I took them to the Madison Club, a private club with stately conference rooms. The service would be impeccable, the atmosphere polished. Afterward, we would enjoy a terrific lunch, beautifully prepared by one of the best chefs in the city. I didn't have a tight agenda, but one goal was to walk out of the meeting with at least a discussion about what we believe to be true—the why behind what we do and why people do business with The Creative Company instead of some other company.

> It's interesting how what we believe can stir up quite a hornet's nest.

On the morning of retreat day, I spent the first two hours of my day working on a client problem. The problem was about a misunderstanding on the bill. I had it documented. He didn't remember. He thought the hourly rate was 50 percent less than what we charged. It was documented—in October—but no, we hadn't reminded him again in March when he needed our help. This is a client for whom we built a $22,000 website. He paid $7,500. A couple of years ago, I sent an employee to the world-class HOW Interactive Design Conference and she came back with this brilliant idea to do flat bids for web projects. We loved it! It would simplify everything. We did these for a year and lost our asses on every single one of them. It's a terrible idea. Don't do it. On this particular day, I felt the sting again. It wasn't just that he didn't remember; it's that I had already paid for the guy's website. As a business owner with kids and bills to pay, this kind of thing isn't just painful for a moment, it stays with you. Nonetheless, the pain put me right back where I was paying for this guy's website. At the time we didn't understand how many things can go off the rails on an e-commerce site.

It was also pouring rain.

But we pressed on.

I made a decision to walk into that room focused on one thing and one thing only—the future. And so we dove in to what we believe:

> We believe the best brands are built from the
> inside out, that great ideas don't come from big cities
> but between your ears, that businesses can do good
> and be good, that words have power, that people are
> the difference maker, that choosing our clients is the
> first step and that saying "no" to some things is more
> powerful than saying "yes" to everything.

Then it happened. One person brought up something ugly from the past. I would tell you what it was exactly but I honestly don't remember because, before she was done, I felt utterly defeated.

This is the reason you should hire a facilitator for your off-site meetings. This is why people hire me. It's because you're just too close to it. There's something that happens psychologically when we're attacked. Fight or flight? Kill or be killed? I decided to wait. I thought about running, though. I honestly did. I felt like I was going to throw up. I was visibly deflated. The employee said, "I ruined our meeting." We all had thought bubbles floating above our heads but no one said a word.

But she didn't ruin the meeting. I really did my best to stay in there and think about what she was saying. Your brain literally stops working when you feel attacked so it took me a minute to get my head back together. Was it right for her to say it with so much emotion that it knocked me over? No. But for the first time I heard it.

She and I, while technically working for the same company, are not having the same experience. She is working for a company where things go wrong every day. In the web world, every single site is threatened every single day. But that's a problem that can sometimes be solved with better security—something clients don't want to pay for or talk about, and that's the other problem. Some clients still think the site is simply a brochure online, so they don't want to acknowledge the potential crisis. Instead, they choose to live in blissful ignorance to the reality that their site may be attacked at any given moment. Sometimes we have to rescue them. When we do, we send a bill that they don't want to pay because they don't understand. Rinse and repeat. It's awful.

In 2009, we built a website for a client. Since then, we have made a few minor updates—less than a grand's worth—but they turned down the maintenance and security agreement, which would have protected them. Their site is old, not old by their terms, but old by web standards. Then what we warned could happen, did happened. The site was hacked—right before the end of the year, when people are giving at record paces. (It's a non-profit.) We rebuilt the whole thing in a matter of days during the holidays. We sent a bill. They paid it. But, this is the world the head of web development at The Creative Company lives in. She's in crisis management every day.

Meanwhile, we're doing a cheese challenge in the PR and social media area for a hipster co-op, talking to the media about the next Dr. Oz and, in general, working on ideas and things that people mostly understand and want to pay for. We're getting great press. We're rocking the numbers for the client. We're watching sales go up and to the right. We manage a crisis PR situation a few times a month but it's not every day and there's a team of us working on it. But my lead developer's like the lone ranger in web. She has support but she knows more than everyone else here. So while we're celebrating, she's putting out another fire. She's frustrated. She's pissed off. If I was having that experience every day, I'd be angry too.

> Sometimes you just need to get it all out on the table.

We've been making moves towards relieving some of the pressure for our web developer and we're continuing in that direction. We've tapped into several other web developers we will be working with so things are in motion, BUT, and this is important—

She just wanted to be understood.

She's a super cool person, very artistic, hard working, brainy and funny. She wears bright tennis shoes almost every day to work and she has a big laugh. People love her. But she thinks people hate her sometimes and that's a problem. There must be a better way to help clients understand the world we live in and the intricacies of what's happening in that space so that the result isn't frustration with the agency that's trying to help them succeed in this world. Right in the middle of this beautiful place, in this great city at our fantastic retreat, there was meltdown of sorts.

It was clearly time to take a break.

So we did what all smart people do at moments like this—we took a bathroom break. We talked about the bees on the wallpaper in the ladies room, and one person said that was normal during the Victorian era. We gave our brains a break. And it worked. We came back to the conference room for the last 15 minutes and summarized what was discussed. The mood was still tense and I started thinking: This is not going well.

Then again, sometimes people just need to be fed. So, we ordered food in the stately dining room from the attentive server and started to settle in. The conversation wasn't where I wanted it, though. We weren't talking about what just happened and everyone was feeling a little nauseous, actually. If you've ever been there, you know what I'm talking about. People start talking about "kids these days" and other safe topics.

Not a great use of our time.

I started it off by saying I think I figured out the problem and, specifically, why it was so frustrating for our senior web developer. It wasn't eloquent but it was out there.

I looked at her and it was like she exhaled and all was right with the world. This woman, who was so frustrated 30 minutes earlier, reached across the table and grabbed my hand. We had a moment, everyone breathed, and then we ate like kings.

The point of my telling you this is to say that retreats are not always smooth sailing. There are going to be some rough and tumble times if you're going to get to the truth of the matter.

In John P. Kotter's book *Leading Change,* he says complacency is the biggest killer of change. When companies are content with the status quo, they don't talk about the hard issues.

Kudos to us. We were fearless. We did the hard thing.

The room lit up again. We talked about the future, the ideas and the new space. We talked about how we're literally going from one side of Madison to the other—almost exactly 180 degrees. We're six blocks from the State Capitol now and we'll be six blocks from the Capitol soon. We're changing.

One person on the team said, "We need a hashtag!"

How about #180in120?

That works!

If you want to transform your company and do a 180 in 120 days—let's talk! As iron sharpens iron . . .

Last but not least, when I thought about the events of our retreat later that night, I was reminded of the scene from *A Few Good Men* where Colonel Nathan Jessup screams, "You can't handle the truth!" at the lieutenant. The truth is, most people can't. It's about ego. It's about us. It's about self-preservation. But in business, it's all about them. It must be. Especially in a professional services firm. If I really want to deliver the kind of service I know we're capable of, I need to get out of the way and really listen.

The truth sets us free. It wasn't easy to get to and I'm a sucker for a pleasant conversation—I really am—but having the tough conversation actually freed us up to move forward. Bring out the microscope. Do the autopsy. Be fearless. Your team, your clients and your community will be better than ever because you had the courage to do so.

Stay tuned. This story is just getting started.

#180in120—The Choice is Yours.
What Will You Do with the Next 120 Days?

How I Lost a Million Dollars

I lost a million dollars seven years ago.

Part of changing this organization in 120 days is getting honest about our history.

So here's the story:

I was working for this terrific client. They were doing $120 million a year in sales. When we met five years earlier, they were doing $60 million. We were named the agency of record.

They loved us. We loved them. They used the Imagine Plan in year two and, together, we took that old and tired company to a whole other level. I loved working on that account. It was visible. The people were cool and, best of all, we had a seat at the table. We were part of the management team—part of the guiding coalition and were knocking it out of the park. They did good things in the community, paid their employees well and for that matter, paid us well.

And then it happened.

They stole my employee.

He wasn't just anyone either. There are some people you can steal from me and I won't care. I cared.

He and I had worked in tandem with each other for five years. We were a great team. He was hard working, smart, and eager. I was the brains behind it. He was the braun. I never had a bad day working with him. Not a single one. He even sent me flowers once—every month—for a year—because I traded vacation time with him. Super classy guy. Really smart. Loved him.

But then he chose something other than me and I was mad.

We didn't have a signed contract with our most fabulous client. I'm not kidding. They were spending $250,000 a year with The Creative Company and we didn't have a signed agreement.

Why? Because I took a vacation.

No joke. Taking a vacation is risky for business owners.

I would tell you why but the truth is, if you're a business owner, you already know. Maybe it's just me but I had a CPA, a VP and a senior account executive who were all working that week and not one of them made sure the contract was signed. Still, my company—my problem.

Five years earlier, I did get another contract signed—the non-compete agreement with the employee.

He came to the hospital to sign it, with me in a hospital gown and everything. I was eight months pregnant and had a tumor the size of a grapefruit outside my uterus. Signed contracts— that's what we do.

But he didn't.

Here's the thing—you really can't make people stay with you who don't want to be with you anymore. Indentured servitude ended a long time ago. You need to let them go do whatever it is they need to do. I didn't like that idea, and wanted things to stay the same. I wanted to do another campaign, go to the recording studio, make another TV ad, and continue the game. But he picked up his marbles, went home with the cool kids with the money, and left me standing all alone.

People don't treat you very well when they've decided they don't want to be in it with you anymore. It's a fact.

In this case, they actually brought me into a conference room— three of them—one who was a former pro football player. They hit a button and shut the shades in the room so no one could see in. It was intimidating, scary as hell, and meant to be. They had millions of dollars and resources and I had enough gas to get home. It really wasn't a fair fight.

Here was the young turk that I had trained, along with the client who I had helped succeed, using tactics to intimidate me. I sat there thinking, "What on God's green earth did I do to deserve this?" In other words, I was feeling sorry for myself and licked my wounds for a long time —probably years— probably up until yesterday even.

We came to a compromise of sorts but I lost $250,000 in

annual revenue that day. Had we continued to work together for another five, well, you can do the math—somewhere between $1.2 and $1.5 million assuming the budget would have grown.

Breaking up is hard to do. But in business, a fair amount of breaking up happens. At the beginning, everyone is all smiles and there are handshakes and checks. It's awesome. Best feeling in the world. Kind of like a first kiss. In the end, they never want to see you again, they don't want to pay the bill, and they unfriend you on Facebook. It's painful.

You can get mad or you can get even, right?

Someone wanted me to meet with their competition afterward. She said, "I told him you would probably want to $^%$ with them." I didn't. I was more interested in winning than getting back. Winning equals fun. Getting back equals an energy drain.

Looking back, I see I had another choice in that conference room. I could have said, "Look, we've done some amazing work together and I want to continue doing amazing things together. This guy has been a great employee and you're going to love him. The dynamic is going to change but let's figure out something that's win-win." Instead, I got mad and told them to take their million dollars and wallow in it. I was taking myself and my car that I bought from them somewhere else—to who knows where but certainly where people appreciated me—and never coming back again. Fare thee well, mates. You're never going to see me again.

And then they closed their doors.

Well, no—that didn't happen. It didn't happen at all. They continued to change, grow, and prosper and are doing fine. At my core, I thought it was about me but it never was—it's always about them—about putting others first and about knowing we're in an ocean where change is necessary for survival and growth. The ocean is alive. It should be respected, valued and appreciated—not because it's always the same, but because it changes.

So what does this have to do with organizational change? Everything. Because until CEOs know why they do what they do and figure out how to do the right thing, their whole team is sunk. We play follow the leader and if your leader is bitter about something that happened in the past, playing the victim, that behavior is going to be part of that organization. You can have one big victim party that smells bad and no one wants to be part of it except other people who are victims. Even if the feeling is not on the surface, it's in the garbage stinking up the whole place.

It's time to take out the trash. We are, and with enthusiasm, I might add. And it's not like your teenage son who really doesn't want to take out the trash, but more like your grandmother who can't stand a smelly kitchen. We're all in.

So how much did it cost to learn this lesson? A million dollars.

Was it worth it? Every red cent.
You better believe it.

> ### #180in120—The Choice is Yours.
> What Will You Do with the Next 120 Days?

Necessary Endings & New Beginnings

Oh—and then this happened.
So yesterday, someone quit.

She was going to leave soon anyway. It was a temporary position but it still stung a little because I didn't know for sure.

Part of being a good boss is that you need to do the exit interview. The exit interview is really about them—not about you. They tell you how screwed up your organization is. It's true—that's what they always do and that's the purpose of the exit interview. Your goal is to have them tell you so they don't feel the need to tell everyone else. It's the smartest thing you can do. But if you built the company from your hands and made sure every check cleared for 26 years, it's not the easiest thing to do.

A side note here—I've had some incredible exit interviews— some which were super helpful and changed our organization for the better. Positive things definitely come from these interviews, so you should do them.

On an employee's first day, she always look great. She smiles at you and says nice things. She tells you how hard she'll work for you. On her last day, she will tell you that your organization is like a three-ring circus and she doesn't want to be in the circus. She will bring up things that happened three months ago while you were in a coma and explain how it wasn't her fault. She will. And you will take it all in.

But back to the story.

I went to the drive-up window at my bank after grabbing a cheeseburger and a chocolate shake from a guy at Culver's restaurant who looked like he understood. I looked at him behind the drive up window and I thought, I bet you have a mostly pleasant job. It reminded me of that scene in *American Beauty* where the executive with the cheating wife and the career that sucks the life right out of him applies for a job at

Mr. Smiley's, a fast-food burger joint. He pulls through the drive-thru smoking a joint and asks for an application. I know that feeling. Anyone who has ever managed anything or had the life sucked out of you starting at the temples and moving throughout your whole body knows that feeling. Kevin Spacey spoke for all of us in *American Beauty.* I gave the movie to my parents, and they thought it was depressing. I thought it was my life—sometimes.

Anyway.

So back to organizational change. One of the things that no one ever tells you when you're changing the direction of your organization is this: Once you get clear about your vision, some people are going to jump ship. It's too hard. They liked the status quo and don't want to do it differently. So they leave. You break up.

But others, people who share your vision, who want to be part of creating something better, and who are about what is possible instead of what has been—they'll stand up taller, dive in deeper, talk about the hard issues, encourage you, lean in and as a member of my team recently said, "boss up." When we get clear about who we are and what we're here to do, those who *aren't* on board go to the background, while those who *are* show up like never before and more people join you—the kind of people you really want working with you.

Once you decide, yes you, the CEO, president, owner, or whatever title you go by, decide to start taking responsibility for everything, people who don't want to take responsibility catch the next train out of town because there are no more victim parties happening.

Business is the most exciting and interesting thing I could have spent my life on.

I love it, but one of the unexpected benefits is that you get to see yourself real every single day. You build the house. In our case, we're tearing it down to the rafters. We are keeping the frame and rebuilding with integrity, character and competency so that this house is not only built on a firm foundation, but built with material that will last.

#180in120—The Choice is Yours.
What Will You Do with the Next 120 Days?

How Jerry Maguire Got It Right

I had a mad crush on Tom Cruise when I was in college. It wasn't his first movie, *All the Right Moves,* that caught my attention—it was *Top Gun.* The uniform. The failure. The comeback. I was drunk with Tom Cruise. So, so cute.

I had to wait for a while to see him again—and I thought—he couldn't possibly, but he did it again—in *Jerry Maguire.* I actually enjoy watching a guy wrestle with emotion and Tom Cruise does it so well. Stoics and/or those who are impossible to read actually bore me. I like to be around people who have something to fight for, someone to love and something to care about.

There are several scenes that stand out in *Jerry Maguire*—the sex scene at the beginning, which is really disturbing in its own way—even he's confused; the scene where he breaks up with his fiancée and she slugs him; and last but not least, the final scene where he says, "You complete me."

Whenever I hear that line, all I can think is, "No, I don't."

No one completes anyone. Hasn't Jerry read *The Missing Piece Meets the Big O* by Shel Silver-stein? You should read this book. It's a children's book and you can find it at your nearest Half Price Books. (Trust me, you'll want to buy it and have everyone you know read it because it makes so much sense.)

Anyway.

I was talking to one of the valued members on my team on

Monday about all the things we're doing at The Creative Company. I showed her a picture I drew of all of our key performance indexes. She loved my drawing. Well, not really because it was just a circle with a bunch of arrows, which is actually my point.

Organizational change doesn't have to be complicated.

She and I started to talk about HOW we could increase just one thing—efficiency.

I asked her: "What slows you down in this place?"

Here's the short list: misplaced files; no paper in the copier; answering phones; administrative tasks; greeting everyone who walks in the door because we're in an open space environment. The list went on and on. She talked for 10 minutes, maybe even 15, without taking a breath.

And then I said, "We need an Amy."

I loved Amy. You would have loved Amy. Everyone here loved Amy. She had little angel wings that she wore to work every day. She flew in and made everything work. It was like magic.

Seriously, like Walt Disney magic. I was always on time; the office ran smoothly; she handed me files as I flew out the door; my travel arrangements were always perfect—everything Amy touched had pixie dust on it and we were all so very happy. She didn't complete me but she was the best assistant I've ever had.

Before coming to Creative Company, Amy was a daycare provider. You wouldn't necessarily think that someone who wrangled kids all day would be a terrific office manager, but that was one of the best hiring decisions I've made. Kid wrangler and office manager—same thing.

She had experience and her bachelor's in communications, which meant she got it—she got what we did, but didn't necessarily want to be in charge of those kinds of things. She did what she did and did it better than anyone ever had before or since.

I bet you're wondering where Amy is now, right?

Well, one day, her daughters' school called and offered her a job—with summers off. She's so smart. She took that job.

I hired someone else. Quickly. Because I was in a hurry. I'm always in a hurry. I've been in a hurry since 1987. It's a fact. I slow down every winter but then I come back again like some sort of hungry lion. It's just my nature. In any case, this nature vs. nurture thing actually gets in my way sometimes, and—

It didn't work out.

The new person was sarcastic, which was attractive in the beginning because I thought she was funny. As it turns out, she really meant it. Who knew? I'm usually the last one to know. I'm too trusting.

So back to hiring an office manager. We started crunching the numbers and here's what we found out.

We determined that it costs each of us at least 2.5 hours a week to do things that Amy had done—probably more—but that equals about $6,000 a month in time that could be billed to a client, or $48,000 a year. With $48,000 a year, we could hire someone and even get a little return on our investment— not immediately—but within a year for sure.

But it gets even better. With increased efficiency in the office, we'll have higher client retention rates.

With higher client retention rates, we lower our cost of new business acquisition. Less business acquisition cost equals more stability, and more stability equals employees staying longer. Employees staying longer means we spend less on hiring and training. See—it's the circle of life. How cool is that?

How did we get there? We thought about it. Sometimes that's all you have to do: turn off Facebook, Twitter, or whatever your social media drug of choice and just think. Thinking is good. Talking is good.

Which brings me back to organizational change and how to increase return on investment. ROI is just one of the KPIs we'll be looking at closely as part of our mission to turn this organization around in 180 days.

Here's what we're measuring:

- Culture
- Client Success
- Net Profit Margin
- Increased Efficiencies
- Email Marketing Engagement
- Increased Influence
- Incremental Sales
- Goal Completion Rate
- Social Interactions

In the next chapter, I'll share what we've accomplished in under 30 days, as well as our goals.

As for Jerry Maguire, I'm a total sucker for a great ending. I don't think anyone completes anyone. It works best if both people in the relationship are whole people. Insecurity breeds fear and mistrust and without trust, as management consultant Patrick Lencioni says, you can't get anywhere.

We have places to go. As do you. We can get there from here. We can and must because the world needs people who give a damn. It just does. On so many levels.

#180in120—The Choice is Yours.
What Will You Do with the Next 120 Days?

What Would Captain Kirk Do?

Does your dad's voice stay in your head? Mine does. I hear him talking to me at least a couple of times a week, even though we haven't lived in the same house in 30 years. I think about my dad a lot in business, actually.

Your dad might have been one of those tender dads who talked to you and went on long walks and read books. Some dads are like that.

My dad worked 12 to 16-hour shifts in a tire factory. He smelled like rubber and sweat when he came home. Talking wasn't high on his priority list.

My dad worked hard for years. He showed me what sacrificial love looks like. He was terrific in his garden, smart with his money, inherently intelligent and good with tools, and he always kept things neat and clean. He told me he would have become a draftsman if he could have gone to college. He built my first drafting tables for The Creative Company. My dad can build anything. He also has Elvis Presley hair. It always looks perfect, even at night and when he wakes up in the morning. I have no idea how he does it. He has better and more hair than most men I know. Here's a picture from last June to prove it.

See—perfect hair.

Anyway, when I was growing up, my dad worked six days a week so he didn't watch much TV. When he did, he watched re-runs of *Star Trek* and

Planet of the Apes. I always wanted to know my dad better, so sometimes I would watch those shows with him—always at a distance of at least four to six feet because he liked his space. Truth be told, I could have cared less about the shows. My dad was a mystery to me, so I would sit and study him. The *Planet of the Apes* show actually scared me and Spock—he scared me too.

But Captain Kirk was another story. Even as a little kid, I liked Scotty the engineer and the helmsmen. But honest to God, they didn't hold my attention. It was Captain Kirk who had it going on.

Captain Kirk was in control. Danger was lurking in every corner of the galaxy but he was on a mission with his team to save the world and his crew on the Starship Enterprise. Do you remember the Captain's Log that ended every episode? When I thought about how I would tell you about everything that's happened in the first 30 days of #180in120, I thought it would be infinitely more interesting if I were able to do it like Captain Kirk.

> *Captain's Log. Stardate 68886.5. The Enterprise is preparing detailed charts of the new system. Although tedious, this effort is the first step toward mastering*

our universe. Traveling at warp speed, we are still five weeks away from charting new territory in sector 600. We are holding position and all main systems are at least temporarily restored.

See? Much more fun. Just reading that, I felt my adrenaline increase. It's like some sort of *Star Trek* endorphin rush. Did you feel it too? I love endorphin rushes, especially when they don't involve exercise. Words do that to me; but then again, I'm wired that way.

I digress.

Back to doing a 180 in 120 days. I'm sure a few of you wondered if maybe it was all smoke and mirrors. Or maybe not. Maybe you're really trusting like me and you thought great things would happen. Well, they have!

Here's what we have to show for our efforts:

Since May 1, 2015, we:
- Held an off-site retreat.
- Invested 60 hours in staff time on planning and process improvement.
- Wrote and published five blog posts

documenting our journey and providing outside accountability. Time invested: 60 hours of staff time (writing, editing, proofing, publishing and distributing through all channels). I write fast. It helps and since we're content creators at The Creative Company—built-in "awesome"—that helps, too.

- Identified key performance indexes to measure.
- Began using Klipfolio, a KPI measurement tool.
- Began working on sales/cost projections with various scenarios for the second half of fiscal 2015.
- Cut costs (vendor, online subscription service, other ancillary services).
- Added two key code development resources to our arsenal, as well as a photo and video studio in Chicago. Initial projects have all happened on time and on budget.
- Started to line up speeches on #180in120.
- Began a partnership with Madison College to help future soloprencurs in the arts be successful, create a feature video workforce for the agency

AND help others live the dream.

- Registered the trademarks for #180in120 for books, consulting, and reserved related URLs.

- Began the process of publishing through Amazon.

- Finalized lease agreement and began planning with the general contractor.

- Engaged with over 20,000 viewers on the blog posts through email, Facebook and LinkedIn with our target audience.

- Re-engaged with several clients who did Imagine Plan within the last decade and are, like me, ready to do it again.

- Increased LinkedIn profile views by 80 percent week over week. I am now in the top 6 percent with my personal connections of over 2,200 people.

You rank in the top 5% for profile views among professionals like you.
#5 out of 99   ▲ 25% in the last 30 days

Like Captain Kirk, I love a good mission. I haven't felt this focused since I wrote and implemented a revised business plan in 2008. It feels really good to get up in the morning excited. I'm not sure how to measure excitement, but I know the result is better performance across the board.

Somebody important said if you don't know where you're going, any road will get you there. Do you know who that was? I don't either. Anyway, that's so true. It's amazing what can happen when you know where you're going.

If you want to watch the old episodes of Star Trek, you can find them on YouTube. If you have any lessons from Captain Kirk you care to share, I'd love to hear them. Here are a few I know for sure:

LESSONS FROM CAPTAIN KIRK

- Know your mission.
- Pay attention to the risks.
- Get your team on board.
- Listen as if your life depends on it.
- Document your progress.
- Be courageous with your words, thoughts, and actions.
- Wear the same clothes every day so you don't have to waste time thinking about things that don't matter.

If you can find a half-Vulcan, half-human to go along for the ride, it will be infinitely more interesting.

Here's to keeping it interesting.

> **#180in120—The Choice is Yours.**
> What Will You Do with the Next 120 Days?

How I Found Out the Real Problem

I love Mondays. I love Mondays because this is when we switch from low gear into high gear and talk about all the work we're

going to accomplish in the coming week.

Since we started doing #180in120, I've added an hour to our Monday morning meeting—at the beginning—to work on strategy. Awesome plan. I'm that boss who invests in my team, asks for input and is highly collaborative. Four gold stars for me. My dad would say, "Don't hurt yourself trying to pat yourself on the back." And Dad, once again, you would be right.

Last week's Monday morning meeting went so well. I had an epiphany the night before that we needed to get to the root issues, which basically has to do with a code of conduct in the office. I found this incredible list and shared it with everyone. I was so excited because I knew it would help me. I thought it would make everyone feel safer at work, trust would grow and incredible things would happen. Here's the list, from evangelist and author Beth Moore.

All of these things will limit your effectiveness in ALL areas of your life:

- Gossip
- Lying
- Profanity
- Perversity
- Rudeness, unkindness, or disrespect
- Criticism
- Breaking a confidence
- Negativism and complaining
- Inappropriate humor, including off-color jokes or humor that demeans people
- Misuse of God's name

One would think these behaviors would not happen within a professional services firm. But they do. I'm as guilty as anyone. We've all become far too casual and it needs to stop because it's just awful.

Like any good and strong leader, I started out by saying, "I need to change. For us to be more effective, I need to clean it up. Can we agree that we all have done some, or most, of these things at one time or another and our code of conduct must be above all of this?"

I work with really smart and awesome people, so naturally, heads nodded in complete agreement.

The Code of Conduct sounded somewhat military-like and, trust me on this, that's not us. I said let's come up with another list. This one is called "House Rules."

On the next page is the first draft of our house rules, which were inspired in part by one of our team member's refrigerator rules for her toddlers.

HOUSE RULES

- Use your words to build others up.

- Help each other as much as you can.

- Treat each other kindly.

- When you're frustrated, talk it out.

- Talk health, happiness, and prosperity to everyone.

- Think only the best, work for the best, expect the best.

- Be so focused on improvement of self that you don't have time to be critical of others.

- Remember the mission.

- Serve well.

- Focus on the solution, not the problem.

- Try to make everyone's job easier.

We then dove head first into client work. Awesome. We're moving in the right direction, right? Yeah, not quite. I noticed something. Somebody at the table wasn't saying much and so I did what any smart boss does: I noted that and thought I would circle back to her later.

We put our focus on the week, the physical move of the location, and all the related details. By all accounts, it was time well spent.

The moving company came to do a walk-thru and provide an estimate in the afternoon. A client stopped by. Normal day by all accounts. I collaborated with somebody on my team about the #180in120 brand look for the blog. All was well.

Toward the end of the day, I asked the person who seemed really quiet why.

And boy did I get an answer.

It turns out that something I said publicly about her several months ago got back to her. It wasn't positive. In fact, it was crushing. Not to get into detail, but there was an email fight. It escalated, I was frustrated and said something I wish I hadn't. I was wrong.

Yup. The boss who is leading change and up to a bunch of good in the world is a hypocrite. I actually said it to her to save her the effort. She was already way out there on a limb.

Now I should say that we all blow it, except maybe those really amazing attorneys I've met over the years. They must have some sort of special training at attorney school that helps them avoid this kind of thing. They always seem to be in control. I'm not. Creative people tend to be more dramatic anyway—either outwardly or through their art—and I'm no exception.

So, way back when, I had said she was dramatic in this interaction with another employee as well as a few other things. Suffice it to say, she said it right back to me and to my face.

This just got real, didn't it?

Later, she said I did a good job staying in there with her and using empathetic statements. I didn't defend myself. I owned it. I read a book called *Crucial Conversations* a few months back and that's what I was plugging into in the moment. I had gone from having a safe and normal convo to a risky one in a matter of seconds. Moments like this can literally determine our fate.

But here's the thing. **She actually did me a HUGE favor.** She let me know, in no uncertain terms, how I had failed her in that moment. And I had.

She also gave me a fair amount of grace, despite the fact that she was spitting nails. She acknowledged she doesn't know what it's like to try to keep this all moving every single day, from a financial perspective or otherwise. She said she appreciated the work, the job and the opportunity. She knows I'm trying to figure it out. She gave me a gift, in reality. A priceless valuable gift. One that very few have cared enough to actually give to me.

Why would I say that? Because most people wouldn't have said anything. They would have quit and moved on, costing us far more. She didn't do it for altruistic reasons or because she's independently wealthy or anything. She needs this job. She did it because it was the truth and she couldn't sit there for one more minute. God bless her.

So here's what I did. I died a little inside as I acknowledged that she was right and then apologized. I felt like running, but stayed. I doubted myself with every fiber of my being. I wondered if I was cut out for this job.

I called my mother and ate something at about 8:00 p.m. I hunkered down with my email and wondered what I was doing. I'm a first-born. We're really hard on ourselves.

I thought I might as well do something for someone else because then I wouldn't feel so aweful. I funded a Kickstarter campaign for my friend Nate Currin. He's so talented and he's created a super cool album called "A Madman & a Poet"—it's about a mountain and the journey. I funded him because I wanted to and also because I needed to do something that would make me feel good. I felt horrible.

I wrote Nate and said he and I aren't that different, even though he writes music, performs and lives in his RV. Yet I run a business, and we're the same, both trying to bring art and commerce together so we can make a living doing what we love, using our gifts to make a difference. We are both performers in some ways—never really knowing if the audience will love us or not. We're both getting up today and trying again because something inside of us says we must. If we don't, something inside of us will die. Even if we fail, at least we do, daring greatness.

Business isn't for wimps, whiners, or people who throw pity parties for an extended period of time. I give myself three or four hours, at most, and then it's time to get back on that horse.

You can probably relate in one way or another, otherwise you wouldn't be reading this.

I did what my mother said I should do on days like this. I went to bed. I woke up the next day, after processing all night long, and wrote this all down.

I'm glad I had the conversation with my team, and learned these things about myself. I asked for it. I really did.

Slow death or deep change—the choice is ours.

What will you choose? I'm choosing to change. The phrase "Be the change you wish to see in the world," often attributed to Gandhi, is right on. Part of being a leader means you get to go first. Lucky me.

#180in120—The Choice is Yours.
What Will You Do with the Next 120 Days?

How to Move People from Here to There

A few years ago, I attended the Global Leadership Summit in Chicago.

For two solid days, I took time to look at my business and important relationships from a completely different point of view—from the top looking down. I had the opportunity to review my work life from a bird's eye view instead of being in the middle where it is hard to see what is going on.

Perspective is mission critical, wouldn't you agree?

Anyone who has ever been inside a corn maze knows that if you can just get on top of the design, you could easily find your way out.

Five years ago, Bill Hybels, author and chairman of the board of Illinois-based Willow Creek Association (WCA), and founder of the Global Leadership Summit, did a talk about moving people from here to there. Even today, it still is one of my all time favorite summit talks I reference.

In any change initiative, there's the beginning where we paint our red-hot vision and there's the end, where people can almost see it. Then there's the middle where things can get a little challenging. How we handle the middle portion of the change "separates the men from the boys," as they say.

The middle of the initiative is where the air is sticky and hot, where people start to get tired, and where the steam can start to run out of the "*Little Engine That Could*."

We are nearing the 60th day of our #180in120 journey and will hit the middle mark in July—the stickiest, hottest month in Wisconsin. I think I may just coast through it on some level because I had the benefit of actually moving physical locations during that time.

Either way, here's what I'm doing—and here's what you can do—to make sure you don't lose steam in the middle of your change initiative.

- **Meet with your team and have a keen eye toward improving processes.**

The overall atmosphere is better at The Creative Company since we started meeting and intentionally listening to one another. I know that sounds really obvious to some of you. If someone had asked me six months ago whether or not we were meeting enough, I would have said "Yes." But our meetings weren't as intentional as they are now. Each week we have daily five- to 10-minute check-ins. One goal of these meetings is to discover everything that's holding us back. In response, I'm trying to use fewer words and listen more carefully. We also have two-hour meetings every Monday to start the week and monthly three- to four-hour off-site meetings at some pretty fabulous places to review our progress on KPIs, brainstorm ideas, and advance plans for The Creative Company.

The important thing is we now have a structure in place we can count on. As a result, people are taking initiative and looking forward to time together.

More than that, whenever there isn't a process in place, somebody jumps on it, adds it to Basecamp (our project management tool), and notifies everyone else. We've gone from complaining about our work to acting on it and changing it—in less than 60 days.

The people who are closest to us matter most.

It's easy to think that the answers are outside of us—out there, some-where—at a conference, Rotary meeting, or a networking event. The fact of the matter is that the people who are closest to us matter most. They just do—so think of that as you're heading out to another fundraiser or networking event. Stop and look around. These people who work with you every day must be first.

Take care of them and they'll take care of clients. That will lead to results and ultimately lead to stronger profitability. If you miss the first step—taking care of those closest who matter the most—you will miss the profitability part. That is the economic engine that fuels everything else.

● Take Time to Celebrate!

Celebrating is also an important part of any change movement. I've discovered that when I'm not so concerned about what's happening out there, but focused on what's happening in here, I  think about the people who work here more. The other day, I brought frozen treats from the Willy Street Co-op to the office after lunch. It's just ice cream but everyone loved it! In addition, I've noticed my team doing more to thank each other—the words we use here have changed over the past four months.

I had to ask, what is the economic value of a changed vocabulary and a more positive outlook in our workplace. I'll tell you in October, but early indications show the needle moving up and to the positive. I also not only remembered somebody's birthday, but I even managed to get a cool card, had it routed around for a signature, and bought her a present. A year ago, I didn't have the bandwidth to celebrate this awesome human's birthday because I was so consumed with serving a client whom I rarely talk to anymore. The project is over and life goes on, but this coworker who continues to be with me through thick and thin is still here and I wanted to celebrate her.

> *The human heart was never meant to handle all of life's disappointments and that is why celebrations are so important.*

So celebrate! Give awards! Make a big deal out of stuff! People love it!

It wasn't that long ago that I felt defeated at times. Each day would bring one more unexpected challenge and there seemed to be no end in sight. I found a quote at the beginning of Robert E. Quinn's book *Building the Bridge As You Walk On It* that resonates with me. It might with you, too:

> *I decided to acknowledge my fears and close off my exits. Suddenly, my workplace became a place filled with people doing their best to either avoid deeper dilemmas or face them and grow. The previous importance of titles and roles began to melt away before my eyes. My own change of perspective led me to see a new organization without having changed anyone but myself.*
>
> *- Jeremy Fish, a doctor based in California*

We are building a productive community—a highly worth-while and even nurturing place. People are more considerate of how their work product affects others. They are each doing their best to make themselves the best they can be, and our culture of success is being strengthened because of it. While we may be approaching the middle mark of change at The Creative Company, I'm incredibly proud of the progress we've made in such a short amount of time.

I'll report back within the next two weeks about where we are, but needless to say, our boat is no longer in the harbor. We are on the open seas and enjoying the experience of sailing this vessel together.

#180in120—We can get there from here!

> **#180in120—The Choice is Yours.**
> What Will You Do with the Next 120 Days?

Because Every New Beginning Is Some Other Beginning's End

July 1

I drove by my childhood home on Saturday afternoon. Until I was eight years old, I lived in a village in northwestern Illinois called Apple River, population 378. Truth be told, that number might be exaggerated. We lived on a small farm on the edge of town where apple trees, gardens, dogs and children all grew together.

Sometimes when I'm stressed, I dream about that farm with the pretty green ferns growing alongside the house. I spent endless days playing in our giant garden, hiding out under the hollowed out tree, playing tag with my cousins, and listening to Puff the Magic Dragon on my record player. That was the place where my mom showed us how to dance to "At the Hop" and we laughed ourselves silly; where we did shadow puppets on the wall; ate popsicles until we were sticky; and caught fireflies until way past our bedtime.

Do you dream about your childhood home?

I hope you do. In my dreams, it will forever be a place filled with wonder.

I needed a place like that in 2008 when I moved my company to the Madison Enterprise Center on Baldwin Street. It was located in the Willy Street neighborhood, an iconic neighborhood with a colorful, bohemian culture.

Do you remember 2008? Sure, you do. We all do. Do you remember what you were doing? If you were like most people, you were panicking. The stock market was going down and the economy was going to hell. People weren't jumping off buildings, but they were thinking about jumping off buildings.

We had done a lot of work for retail brands up to that point, but people weren't buying cars and jewelry like they were a few years before.

That wasn't the only thing that was changing.

The way we consumed media was about to dramatically shift, too. I started to look around and took inventory. TV, radio, print, and billboards had brought us this far, but the internet had changed everything. Suddenly, each person had the potential to BE the media.

When I started the company, four TV stations and PBS ruled the air. Now, there are hundreds. My copywriter didn't even listen to local radio stations because he had—you guessed it—satellite radio—and looked at all of us like we were stuck in the dark ages.

So in the midst of major change, I chose to change, too.

I rewrote the business plan to focus on new media—social media, web development, email marketing, and art and design—all built around a story worth caring about. I needed a place to land with all of these new offerings, where we could hunker down and learn. The MEC provided that place.

It was risky. Seven years later, I can say I knew what I was doing, or we did; but we really didn't. No one ever really knows when he or she is speculating about the future. It could have bombed, but didn't. That was good.

Anyway, we came to this vacant space and it was literally a giant box of possibility. The walls were a dingy white. Somebody made t-shirts in this space before we arrive. It wasn't pretty, but my art director said, "I think we can make it work."

He was right.

We could make it work.

It's kind of like when your parents look at your starter home and say, "It has potential."

That same feeling—but we dove in.

I lost money in 2008.

I also liquidated everything I could to keep it all moving. And

then there was the
divorce. As my
mom would say,
things could only
get better. I may
have been talking
business, but I was
dying inside. After
nearly twenty years

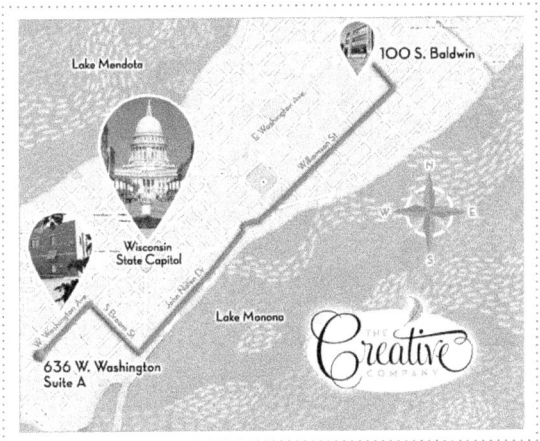

in business, my plane was running on fumes. We were also in
the midst of an almost unprecedented economic downturn. I
was also in a personal crisis of some magnitude. However, this
place gave me a runway to safely land my plane with the cast
and crew intact.

A year after we moved to the MEC, we planned to host a
party for all of our new neighbors and Downtown Madison,
Inc. We were mostly working hard and the walls still weren't
painted. Friends stepped up though. Like magic, an interior
designer came through the door followed by a painter with
an amazing crew of painters. Not too long after that, the guys
from Coyle Contract installed new flooring in the front of the

office. Have you ever had friends that just show up to help? Yet, we had something that makes all the difference in the world.

We had hope.

We practically wrote the word on a balloon, tied a string on the end, and held on to it with all our might while working day and night and night and day—and we laughed. We laughed our way right out of that damn recession and the most miserable year of my life.

Last year, my neighbor had cancer and his buddies all showed up to shovel his driveway. I thought it was the most beautiful thing ever. It was the same when my friends showed up. I didn't have cancer but I definitely needed help. Friends make the world go round. Together we added touches of whimsical creativity

here and there, and this old and tired industrial space breathed new life. Some even said it had a *je ne sais quoi* quality about it. It was captivating and alluring. The world outside may have been brutal, but in this place, everything was possible.

In this place, everything was possible.

It's a different time and a new day at the agency. We're ready for the next chapter in the story.

It is, dare I say, more professional at our new location? I think the MEC will stay with me for a very long time—like the childhood farm. I may even drift off to sleep sometimes remembering this place where we played Sinatra on the CD player, and wowed clients with our wickedly good imaginations. It was a place where the only thing between us and meeting payroll was the next client who walked through the doors. We danced through the recession. and daydreamed our way right out of it as only artists and a renegade bunch of hard-working creative people can do.

My art director from 2008 went off to do other wonderful

things at his own online company, but others remained in one way or another. I wouldn't want to do it again, but we've been tried, tested, and adapted to skills we didn't have before. I'm grateful for every small act of kindness, as well as every client who hired us to handle the new media landscape without really knowing the outcome. Still, they trusted our vision along the way. It paid off for the early adopters and here we are again, pioneering a new frontier with content marketing and online publishing. I don't know where we'll be in 2022, but I do hope, wherever it is, we're still using our imaginations and knowledge to get from here to there. I've found those two things can do more than keep the lights on—they keep the ideas flowing. Where there are great ideas, there's life.

Sixty days into the change initiative and we're deep into "Kotter's 8-Step Process for Leading Change" plan. It is quieter here, more oriented towards process and productivity. We're prepared for a tremendous second half of the year.

Goodbyes are hard to say. I have a hunch I'll have a "moment" when I turn in the keys next week and do one final walk-through at the old office. You probably know what I mean. If you've lived at all, you've said goodbye to places and people you've loved. It hurts a little—even if you know where you're going will be filled with its own stories and adventures.

A few years ago, there was a popular song called "Closing Time," by Semisonic. I heard an interview with the writer of the lyrics (and the leader of the band) who said it's actually cleverly disguised as a bar song. The fact of the matter is—he wrote the song when his son was born. It seems to be an ending, (hence the title), but as he writes, it's actually a beginning. "Every new beginning comes from some other beginning's end." There's a sadness that inevitably comes from saying goodbye to the things we love and are familiar with—jobs, companies, clients, colleagues—but there is a whole world out there that is filled with possibility.

#180in120—Yes, you can get there from here.

#180in120—The Choice is Yours.
What Will You Do with the Next 120 Days?

Why I Want to Be a Cowboy

July 24

Do you want to be a cowboy? I want to be a
cowboy. If you're in business, you could be a cowboy.
A cowboy is a man with guts and a horse. I'm a woman, but I
have guts and I could probably get a horse if I needed to.

I'm reading a book about cowboys now. I bought it this week at Half Price Books. It's called *How Successful People Win*. The author is Ben Stein. It was $9.95.

I want to win and had 10 bucks, so I thought I should probably buy the book. Plus, the author uses cowboys as a role model. Who doesn't like a good cowboy story?

It turns out Ben's life was going nowhere until he decided to think like a cowboy. He worked in a depressing neighborhood in a big city where people hung out in dark corners and drank too much. His office was in a converted supply closet. None of his friends were going anywhere either, and would get together and talk about how miserable life was.

He was approaching 30 and realized he was dying.

He couldn't quit his job because he didn't have enough money to quit his job. Then, one day, he realized he was in so much pain that he couldn't take it any longer. He was a prisoner on death row who had nothing to lose by trying to break out.

So he broke out.

Ben started studying successful people and doing what they do. It worked and Ben's life started to change. He's a lawyer, economist, writer, actor, teacher, and former game-show host.

When I first started my business, I was in a basement in an old office building. Eventually, I moved into a converted warehouse. I paid $160 a month and shared a reception-ist with a dozen other small businesses. She was no ordinary receptionist—she wore high heels and played odd pranks on people. I was afraid of her. Still, the price was right. I think I paid an extra $20 for her to answer my phones, which was risky. Mostly, I answered the phones. A pest control company was across the hall from me, and Nathan from Critter Control was next door. This was my glamorous life in advertising. I sold ad campaigns for a song to a resale store, a diner, and a carpet store—all of which are out of business now. Sometimes I would have lunch at this bar nearby with a friend. I ate the chili and cornbread as if it was sustenance to my soul, because it was. This was not how I had always imag-ined it would be. This cowboy was dying, too.

Somewhere in the mid-90's, I moved into a nicer space on Madison's D'Onofrio Drive and landed a telecommunications client. This was 1996, so the Telecommunications Act was creating massive changes. This was good for me because they started to recognize marketers as more than just another commodity. On top of it, they were great people. The checks were decent. Plus, they had "street cred," which gave me "street cred," which meant I had a shot.

I moved my business five times in my first 10 years of business. You have to keep moving when you're a cowboy. If you're driving through the range and there's no water in sight, you had better keep moving or your herd will die. I always kept moving. Clients came and clients went. I didn't sit around and lick my wounds for too long because I couldn't afford to.

I sat next to the CEO of the largest commercial lender in Wisconsin yesterday at Downtown Rotary. He asked, "What's the secret to staying in business for 25 years?" I said, "I always had enough money to go one more day." Of course, it's more complex than that but there's some truth to it, too. I just kept going—even when, even if, even though.
I didn't quit.

Every day, there were risks though—thieves, wolves, weather, and internal threats. It's still that way.

The West may be yours but there's a million ways to die in the West, too.

My kids actually took me to that movie, *A Million Ways to Die in the West*. They told me it wasn't "that bad." It was a Saturday night. I let them pick. They are teenagers so I can trust them, right? It really *was* that bad. You shouldn't take your kids to it. I was just hoping no one saw me in there. At one part I had to put my hands over my son's eyes.

The trailer will make you laugh, though. Find it online and watch it even if you're really busy. Laughing actually increases creativity.

And here's the thing—there are a million ways to die in the West. Same in business. A million ways to die. So, why do it?

Because every cowboy knows that to get what you want in life, you have to leave your bunkhouse. There's really no better feeling in the world than being out in wide open spaces knowing it's yours to win or lose.

Here's what happened when I left my bunkhouse over the last few weeks:

- I landed a new client—that was good.
- A potential client went to a conference and came back and decided not to do a $25,000 campaign.

He realized he was pushing his team too much. That was bad for me, not them. Well, maybe them. Time will tell.

- Someone said "the check was in the mail," but it never came.
- A competitor wanted to have lunch.
- A competitor gave me a lead.
- A competitor offered a job to one of my employees and the employee took it.
- A national company asked me to blog for them.
- A client thanked us for all our hard work and gave us more.
- A client renewed our contract.
- A long-time client stopped responding and their credit card was declined.

This is business.

Good things. Bad things. When you're a cowboy, it's all in a day's work. You know how to rope, wrangle, herd, cut, cull, and so on. The trick is, you must be able to endure the constantly changing environment of a cowboy and see challenges not as an enemy, but something to triumph over.

Excuses are the enemy, and we are the ones making excuses.

Is it a failure or a success when things happen? I don't know. I do know if I spend too much time thinking about it and have a sense of failure around it, my self-esteem is hurt. Low self-esteem leads to unhappiness. As Ben Stein says, "Low self-esteem and unhappiness are the two ineluctable handmaidens of a wasted life." And because I'm the leader and everyone follows the leader, I had better lick those wounds and get back on that horse again so we can make it to our destination.

A cowboy doesn't get up in the morning and feel sorry for himself, complain about everything, say no all day to every request, and hope somehow that his cattle get to their destination. No, a cowboy leaves the bunkhouse ready for action. He gets everything he wants by moving, minimizing threats and pressing toward getting to his destination. He has a great attitude and a high sense of self. He achieves the goals he sets before himself.

That is why I want to be a cowboy. I read this on the Oklahoma state website and thought it was worth sharing. They have a quiz you can take, too. It's fun, and it turns out that I'm 90 percent cowboy. Anyway, here's their definition of a cowboy:

" BEING A COWBOY
isn't in your clothes. It's in your character.

It's the passion to do what's right even when it's hard. It's ending the day knowing you gave it everything you had. It's standing out by standing tall.

It's integrity. And honor.

And courage to see hope even when you're the only one who sees it. "

#180in120—The Choice is Yours.
What Will You Do with the Next 120 Days?

How to Succeed in Business—Choose Yourself

September 15

On May 1, 2015, I decided enough was enough and we embarked on #180in120 and a commitment to improving things— not just a little, but a lot. It was time to shift this baby into gear and make something happen. I gave myself 120 days—until August 31.

Cruise control is boring. I once wrote a client of mine and

said I was bored. He hired me to do a $100,000 project. Best time of my life. I had purpose, meaning, and people to do it with. I was on a mission. Life was great. But this time, the status quo was our daily companion for far too long.

Owning a business, serving others and leading people require far more of us than we could even begin to imagine. On any given day, a whole lot isn't in our control. Not only were we on cruise control, but some attitude shifts needed to happen, too—across the board and beginning with us.

I own a book called *The Mathematics of Marriage.* It's a textbook for psychologists. I still haven't read the whole book. I bought it because of one simple idea. The idea is that all relationships are mathematical and are similar to a bank account. The deposits must outweigh the withdrawals or the relationship will fail. The author and psychologist, John Gottman, has found that marriages fall into the danger zone for divorce when the ratio of positive to negative interactions falls below five to one. If you remember just one thing from reading this book—remember this point—5 to 1. That's the secret. Hit that number and you will be golden. Miss it and that relationship will go south.

In my business, the negatives had outweighed the positives for six to nine months. Little, but annoying things, are not great to deal with. Eventually, I just had to say enough. Let's do something about it together. A hundred percent accountability is a tremendous motivator.

I needed to do something different. Twenty-five years at the helm is a long time. Frustration and boredom had taken root. In the spring, I took time to write and think. I spent some time with people I admire just because I love to spend time with them—not because we had business to discuss. I stopped "doing" long enough to ask myself and others some questions. I've learned so much since then, and I hope by sharing it with you that your life, your business and your work will be better for it.

The honest to God truth is—I didn't know where it would land.

#180in120 was born out of the decision to work the problem until the positives outweighed the negatives.

I am, after all, 100 percent responsible.

I started by doing some things that were scary. One was actually taking the time, by myself, to write down what I loved and what I didn't enjoy about this business. I also spent some time playing with ideas and thinking about people Steve Jobs called "the crazy ones," the ones who see things differently.

I thought about the many things that make me want to get up in the morning and wondered how I could bring more of that into my business life again.

I thought about the things that drain me, cause problems, cost money, and how I could remove those from my business.

I told all of you what I was up to, as well as my employees, so I had 100 percent accountability from every corner.

Creating a "Yes, and ..."culture

I also began to spend more time with people who are successful and who believe and act in a way that creates success. I began to create a culture that says, "Yes, and" instead of "We can't because ..." I moved far, far away from the naysayers, the critics and the haters. Or they moved away from me. I'm not really sure which came first, but the people in my life changed. I did speaking engagements and panel discussions with people who live in the world of possibility and action.

I closed that door quietly and respectfully and moved toward something better for me and my company. It took time, but real change didn't happen until I decided it had to. Small changes daily lead to big changes over time.

A major impetus of this change was a man I've yet to meet. His name is James Altucher. He's transparent, smart, and funny. He has taught me so much this summer. James Altucher's blog is one you should absolutely read. He's fearless in his commitment to helping you choose yourself. It sounds selfish, but it's not. It's really about figuring out what makes you come alive and then going and doing it. If you've ever spent time with someone who is bored, frustrated or angry with their work, you're already tracking with me.

I did a fair amount of management consulting work before the recession knocked the wind out of me and the rest of the world. So I brought out Kotter's eight-stage process of change, dusted off the cover and dove in. I think the most important changes were in me, though. By writing my ideas down, taking time to think, choosing to get closer to my clients and employees, and ultimately choosing myself first, I was able to be more productive and more satisfied. My life is infinitely better than it was a year ago. My work is better. My company is better. Better is good.

So what happened in 120 days?

Here's the short list:

- I fell in love again with what I do. I think this is the most important thing of all. I also began to have a much clearer understanding of my own gifts, contributions and motivations. Everything else falls into place once you answer that question.

- We measured culture, client success, net profit margins, increased efficiencies, incremental sales, goal completion rate, social interactions and email marketing engagement. Without exception, we improved in every area, generally in the double digits.

- We cut expenses on everything from IT to software to cleaning expenses. We're operating leaner than a year ago, while simultaneously investing more in the things that actually give us a strong ROI, including client services and marketing. We held several off-site company retreats and dinners with clients. Best of all, I am pleased to report our net income is considered the gold standard for agencies our size. We experienced a nine-point increase in net profit in just four months.

- I went from the top 10 percent to the top one percent for professionals like me on LinkedIn. I like winning and I love showing that social media works. I was able to achieve both goals with these metrics. I published nine posts in all during the 120 days. Pulse is one of the best tools available on the web. Work it. Tell your story. Write about things that matter. Being a thought leader draws people in.

- Referral, organic, email and direct traffic to our website was up 341 to 471 percent over a year ago—and people, it was summertime in Wisconsin.

- I legally trademarked #180in120, secured my ISBN number for publishing the book on change later this year and wrote the marketing plan for incorporating management consulting and strategic planning into what we do at The Creative Company.

- We began the process of rebranding The Creative Company.

- We added 900 subscribers to our email list, an increase of 21 percent. We sent 11 campaigns over the last four months, compared to three the previous summer. Our reach was four times greater.

- We wrote a business plan for the next three years. I had written a plan every year for the last seven years and we experienced very steady growth. However, I hadn't planned beyond that year. I'm a big advocate of "Where there is no vision, the people will perish." Just knowing we're thinking about 2020 helps shape decisions today.

- We moved west: well, 16 blocks west but still, we moved. It's quieter, more professional, closer to the University of Wisconsin campus and downtown. We landed several terrific new clients in areas where I know we'll shine, so they'll shine.

- I landed a number of speaking engagements: United Way Leadership Council, the Wisconsin Institutes for Discovery, American Family's DreamBank, and Periscope for Web Developers and Designers at Filament Games.

- I was invited to blog for the Better Business Bureau Serving Wisconsin and to join Madison College's visual arts track advisory board. This will give us access to talent and give students access to real-life experiences.

- We improved processes across the board, resulting in higher gross profit margins and stronger client and employee satisfaction.

- I hired an office manager/executive assistant. I wrote about why we needed one earlier in the summer. Thinking and planning leads to action and results.

So, what happens next? We do it all again—that's what happens! Before the recession in '08, we wrote five-year business plans, right? While that's still important. I think it's just as important, if not more so, to keep you and your team focused on what you're doing today to make your company better.

My cyber mentor, James Altucher, says it's a one percent game. One percent better every day means a 365 percent improvement in a year. I've bought in and it's paying off for me. I hope it does for you, too.

So what do you think? Does my experience help you focus on your change? What did you learn?

Share your stories by emailing me at
laura@thecreativecompany.com
or by messaging me on LinkedIn.
You can also follow me on Twitter
@creativecompany

#180in120—The Choice is Yours.
What Will You Do with the Next 120 Days?

Postscript:
Why It's Better to Be Brave

November 6, 2015

I was on the East Side of Madison this morning and stopped to take this picture. It caught my attention because it's a door that goes to nowhere. It's just there. I wondered—what happened to the stairs? Had there ever been stairs? And what happens if you're living inside and you sleep walk right outside and land on your head? It could happen. It looked odd, dangerous and compelling all at once.

You probably don't stop to take pictures of doors that go nowhere. I do. I try to capture everything because I see stories everywhere I look. Sometimes it's hard to be in my head. Sometimes I think too much. Sometimes people even tell me "you think too much." If you think too much, you already know what I mean. If you don't, lucky you! We should hang out sometime.

In business, I'm always thinking—thinking about where the client will be in six months, a year or longer. I have to think about all the steps that we'll have to take to get from here to there. I think about my client's customer or donor, or all the people we'll need to mobilize and focus to get the job done. Plus, I think about a million other people who will or will not be impacted by the effort. I think about everything. I'm the visionary, the master planner, the one who brings it to life. Thinking is my business.

So I see this door and I'm thinking about all the doors I've walked through in my life. I'm asking questions, too, like why is that door just going nowhere?

Why wasn't it turned into a wall? Why did they keep it? What does it look like on the other side? These are questions with no evident answers.

I remember my very first offices—and the door to get in. It was in a basement of a decent office building and I had half windows. My rent was $350 a month. The year: 1989. I put inspirational signs from David Ogilvy on the door every day for my staff of college students so they would be inspired. I was broke most days, so all I had to give anyone was inspiration and friendship. You get very good at friendship when that's all you have to give.

One day, a man on the third floor (higher rent) walked through the door and gave me a book with a title, "Confessions of an SOB". I never did read it. I thought he was cynical. He probably was, but I bet he had a lot of money when he retired. He was that kind of guy. I wasn't that kind of person, though. That book bugged me. Success isn't measured that way, at least in my book.

Sometimes I remember the first day I interviewed someone and made a hire. Over the years, I bet there have been hundreds of people I have interviewed. I don't count. But I remember many of them. I remember the characters most of all. They capture your attention and your imagination. I remember the guy who wore flip flops to the interview, and the woman who wore a sparkly short skirt and asked for $120,000 a year. She had worked for a dotcom with inflated salaries and other people's money. I hope she found a job that paid that well. I learned a lot that day. I was glad I had to be scrappy, for one, and glad I was never so bold as to not have a grasp on reality.

I remember Peter. He was an intern who worked here for a few weeks. His first responsibility was to hang Christmas lights over the sprinkler system. I think he started planning his exit strategy immediately. He wanted to write. He's probably writing novels now. I'll probably have to hang his Christmas lights someday. For now, I still take out the garbage, hang Christmas lights and ask other people to do those things, too.

I remember when our former art director, Mauro Magellan, walked through the doors of the agency for the first time. He was a drummer with the Georgia Satellites, with chart topping songs like "Keep Your Hands to Yourself."

He was a designer, too. He was so genuine and truly a cool cat. We had met only briefly once. Then one day he just walked into The Creative Company and asked for a job. He was so bold, audacious and honest. You would have hired him, too. I said, "yes"—pretty much on the spot, as I recall—and we collaborated on a number of campaigns. It was good. It was somewhat unexpected and it honestly worked.

Why is it that sometimes you can spend months trying to find the right candidate and come up with zip, while other times the right person just walks through the door at the right time and you're set?

Sometimes it's because someone walked through the door at the right time. Sometimes it's because you walked through the right door at the right time.

Mauro, eventually started spending more time in Europe, as rock star artists do, and left the agency through the same door he came through.

I have faced doors that lead to nowhere, just like the one in the picture. It's funny how I don't remember those as well, though. The ones I remember most are the ones through which we went on adventures together and created notewor-thy work and built something worth talking about.

I'm usually a little nervous the first time I walk through a door. You're probably not because you're super secure. But I always want the client to like me and hire us. I always hope they'll be nice, respond to my emails and be kind to the people I work with. I hope we'll have fun together, do great work and care about each other. I hope that if I have a bad cold one day, and I'm not my normal inspiring self, that they'll remember they get colds and not be mad, just because I'm human. And I really hope to God they'll pay their bills. My least favorite thing is chasing after money. But working with people who answer your bids for attention, collaborate well and get things done is the best stuff of life. Sometimes that happens, and sometimes it doesn't. I wish I always knew which doors to walk through.

But I never do. I never know for sure. I just have to be brave and walk through the doors—each and every one.

Sometimes there's magic on the other side like on a game-show. Other times, it simply works well enough. Then there are times when the door opens and you land on your head in the parking lot because that door leads to nowhere.

You need to be brave and keep walking through the doors anyway. Mark Twain is often quoted: "Twenty years from now you will be more disappointed by the things that you didn't do than by the ones you did do."

I've walked through doors that disappointed me, but there are many more I've walked through that I wouldn't trade for anything.

The first time I went to New York City, I stayed at the infamous Hotel Chelsea. I'll never forget the first time I walked through the doors.

The lobby of the Hotel Chelsea, in New York City.

This is where artists, authors, drug dealers, musicians and prostitutes stayed in the 1960's. Bob Dylan, Arthur Miller, Madonna and Janis Joplin all stayed there. Sixty percent of the hotel was for permanent residents, their birds and small dogs. I felt like I was living in a movie. I shared a bathroom with other guests. Every day I was glad I lived to see the next. A radiator went off all night. It was a seedy hotel.

I was there to judge national advertising awards for the Retail Advertising and Marketing Association, a division of NRF. There were a few really creative campaigns and a whole lot of advertising circulars. But it was in Soho, my art director was into it and I had never been to New York City. I was 40 years old. It was the height of the recession, but I thought for sure that if I went, I would meet some great people in the industry who would hire us. No one hired us. I lost money that year—not a lot, but some. I would have lost less if I hadn't gone to New York, but then I wouldn't have the story.

I got to walk through Central Park and see Macy's at Christmas. I got to escape for a few days to a different world. I walked through Hell's Kitchen at 1 a.m. and ate a hot dog.

I rode the subway at odd hours and smiled at dogs and people. I listened to jazz at the Blue Note club. When I was in Little Italy getting gelato, a big Italian guy in a white stretch limo asked my art director and me if we wanted a ride back to the hotel for $20, and we took it. We didn't die and I got to walk through doors I had only read about in books. Awesome.

I was brave.

This is why I started playing piano at Downtown Rotary in Madison recently. It scares me to death every week I do it but I do it anyway. Downtown Rotary is a big deal. We're one of the largest service clubs in the world, and the room is filled with people who create change in the world. I was recruited to play a month ago by a former surgeon. I didn't think I'd actually play for a while. But the next thing you know, I'm on the schedule, all because I walked through a door. I didn't know exactly where it would take me, but I walked through it just the same. I like it because it causes me to stretch.

I'm meeting all kinds of new people because I was brave enough to get up there and try. And by no means am I doing it perfectly. I'm the best they've got and I'm willing. Every week, there are over 225 Rotarians who want to sing a patriotic song and Happy Birthday. I help make it possible, even though I'm scared out of mind each time I do it.

I'm also demonstrating, to the best of my abilities, that you can do something just for the love of it even if you don't do it brilliantly. I hope that takes the pressure off everyone else in the room. I'd like to think it does.

Somebody actually offered me medicinal pot the other day. He's kind of a big deal so it surprised me, but it also told me a lot about what's happening out there—people are freaking out every day. The pressure is real and we're probably not going through enough doors that really make us happy. I turned him down, by the way, but I was flattered he thought I might smoke pot. I'm honestly not that cool—never was, never will be. I have asthma and, in general, avoid things that smoke.

I don't know what's going to happen tomorrow for you, me or any of us. I only know that the doors we walk through make our lives infinitely more interesting. I would prefer not to walk through the ones that go nowhere or where I could get hurt, but that's a risk every single time. What does it cost to go through only the doors where we know what's on the other side? By avoiding the ones that drop us on our heads, we also avoid the ones that will cause us to stretch, grow, be changed or be happy. We might miss the friendships, adventures, rich experiences and newness of trying something we've never done before.

Be bold. Be audacious. Be brave. Be yourself and for the love of Mike, live. Walk through as many doors as you can. Even if you get dropped on your head, you'll still have the story about the time you almost died, but instead, you lived to try again.

> **#180in120—The Choice is Yours.**
> What Will You Do with the Next 120 Days?

RESOURCES

Leading Change, by John P. Kotter
www.kotterinternational.com

The Missing Piece Meets the Big O, by Shel Silverstein
www.harpercollins.com/9780060256579/the-missing-piece-meets-the-big-o

Klipfolio.com
www.klipfolio.com

Crucial Conversations: Tools for Talking When Stakes are High,
by Joseph Grenny, Ron McMillan, Kerry Patterson, Al Switzler
www.mhprofessional.com

Willow Creek Association (Global Leadership Conference)
www.willowcreek.com

Building the Bridge As You Walk On It: A Guide for Leading Change,
by Robert E. Quinn
www.wiley.com/WileyCDA/WileyTitle/productCd-078797112X.html

How Successful People Win: Using "Bunkhouse Logic" To Get What You Want In Life,
by Ben Stein
www.hayhouse.com/how-successful-people-win

The Mathematics of Marriage, by John M. Gottman, James D. Murray, Catherine
C. Swanson, Kristin R. Swanson, Rebecca Tyson
mitpress.mit.edu/books/mathematics-marriage

James Altucher's blog: www.jamesaltucher.com

*Photo Credit: Chelsea lobby by Historystuff2/Own work. Licensed under CC BY 3.0 via
Wikimedia Commons: commons.wikimedia.org/wiki/File:ChelseaLobby.JPG#/media/
File:ChelseaLobby.JPG*